# SOMERSET
in the
OLD DAYS

## DAVID YOUNG

First published in 1984
by Bossiney Books
St Teath, Bodmin, Cornwall.
Designed, printed and bound in
Great Britain by A. Wheaton & Co. Ltd, Exeter.

To Geoffrey Bullivant

## ACKNOWLEDGMENTS

Acknowledgment and grateful thanks for permission to reproduce photographs are due to the following people and organisations: L.E.J. & M.A. Brooke Photographic and Postcard Collection; Terry Brown, Studio 14; Cressrelles Publishing Co. Ltd; Exeter Maritime Museum; Marion Felix; Mildred Ford; Doris Frances; Nicholas J.W. Gaffney; Robin Harvey Photographic Collection; L.C. Hayward; Brenda Herrin; Sydney Hyde; Brian Jackson Photographic Collection; D. Kettlety; Peter Perkins Photographic & Postcard Collection; Pendella Studios, Plymouth; Raneleigh Press; B.G.L. Rendall; R.C. Riley Photographic Collection; Dorothy A.M. Squibbs; Television South West; H.C. Tilzey; Westland Aircraft Co. Ltd; Yeovil Museum Picture Collection. I am also grateful for permission to use illustrations from the following books: *The Book of Yeovil* by Leslie Brooke; *Yesterday's Yeovil & Its Traders* by Leslie Brooke and *The Romans at Ilchester, Lufton, Yeovil & District* by L.C. Hayward, B.A., B.Sc., F.S.A. Finally, my sincere thanks go to Brian Jackson for his invaluable help in the preparation of the transport section and to Paul Honeywill for colouring of the cover.

## About the Author and the Book

David Young is one of the best-known faces and voices in the whole of the Westcountry through his role as Television South West's roving architect. Though a professional architect he spends the greater part of his time writing and broadcasting about his favourite subject: buildings, ancient and modern.

The youngest past Chairman of the Education Committee on Somerset County Council, he is passionately interested in all subjects relating to the Westcountry. Parents of three grown-up children, David Young lives with his wife, Margot, a radio actress formerly with *The Archers*, and their various animals in Yeovil, but he travels throughout the whole South Western region making his television programmes.

In 1983 he made his debut as a Bossiney author with *Around Glorious Devon* in which he takes readers on a personally-conducted tour of his glorious Devon beginning at B for Bickleigh and ending at Y for Yealmpton. More recently he contributed a chapter to *Sea Stories of Devon*.

Here in *Somerset in the Old Days* David Young provides the text for a rich harvest of old Somerset photographs and picture postcards. His words and the skilful old photographers combine to turn the calendars back. For the older generation this book is an opportunity to travel down memory lane and for the younger generation it takes us back in time and mood to a vanished – or vanishing – Somerset.

# Somerset in the Old Days

Somerset is various things to different people, but one thing is sure: no true traveller can possibly be disappointed. Rural tranquillity, contrasting farmland, cream teas, Cheddar cheese and, of course, cricket and cider: Somerset boasts all these – proudly and rightly so – but it is so much more.

*Below:* Summer 1916 at Weston-super-Mare.
*Right:* Bridgwater in the late 1860s.

This Somerset landscape is saturated in romance and history. These hundreds of thousands of Somerset acres range from huge landscapes to dominating heights, from parkland that can only be Somerset to winding country lanes. It can offer the bustle of business and industry or isolation and solitude. It is a place to stir the imagination.

These old photographs turn the calendar back as nothing else can. For the older generation who knew Somerset in the old days, they are a chance to travel down

Tarr Steps – a clapper bridge on Exmoor. Flat slabs about seven feet long rest on piers laid on the river bed. It is thought to date from the Bronze Age.

memory lane, and for the younger generation they take us back in time and mood to a vanished – or vanishing – Somerset.

Somerset was sadly truncated by Local Government boundary reform in 1974; a boundary change which I deplore and intend to ignore for, after all, these photographs were taken long before the county's tragic mutilation.

Think of Somerset as crescent-shaped, bordered by the Mendip Hills, the Quantocks and Exmoor, with the Somerset Levels forming the heartland of the county, draining into Bridgwater Bay and the Bristol Channel. This flat central area was originally a large shallow sea inlet which silted up over a period of several thousand years, forming a huge plain just a few feet above sea level. Today much of the area is still a labyrinth of willow-lined drainage ditches known as rhines.

It took many thousands of years for acid peat bogs to form and today peat is extracted on quite a large scale. Rarely is it used now for burning on hearths for it is far more valuable to gardeners and agriculturalists.

Many prehistoric remains have been preserved in the peat, not least of which is the 'Sweet Track' near Westhay. Thought to have been the earliest trackway in the world, it was a kind of plank walk built across the swampland at least 6,000 years ago. Nearby at Meare and towards Glastonbury you can find grassy mounds which mark the positions of what are often referred to as 'lake villages', which were actually lakeside settlements amidst the then swampy ground. Even earlier man found it safer and more comfortable to live in the limestone caves of the Mendip Hills and prehistoric forts and barrows cover many of the hills.

*Right:* Pulteney Bridge, Bath, built in 1770 by Sir William Pulteney to Robert Adam's design – unique in Britain as it has shops on both sides.

So the nature of Somerset's topography is divided into two quite distinct terrains, from which two quite different styles of living developed. Without doubt, life was harder on the vast waterlogged plain; there was little in the way of protection from one's enemies, other than building your home in a defensive position on an island, whilst surrounded by an abundance of just two meagre commodities – water and withies.

Meanwhile on the hills man lived in comparative luxury, tending his livestock and preparing cloth from the wool of the sheep.

Exmoor National Park lies to the west of Taunton, the county town, and the atmosphere of its 250 square miles has been vividly captured for all time in R.D. Blackmore's famous novel *Lorna Doone*. It

It is good to know that some things survive against all odds. The rare picture (*right*) shows Brunel's steam dredger, built in Bristol in 1844, at work on the River Parrett near Bridgwater. Happily she is still in one piece for us to see preserved for all time and, as you can see (*below*), still afloat at the Exeter Maritime Museum.

Dedication of the Temple at Bath about A.D. 160

This postcard – from a rare set issued in 1910 as part of the Bath Historical Pageant – illustrates the dedication of the Roman temple about 160 AD.

stretches to the coast where it nose-dives into the sea from a height of 1,000 or more feet, probably the highest cliffs around the English coast.

It is generally thought that the name Somerset is derived from the *Somersaetas*, the summer folk, Saxons who settled here during the summer months and eventually stayed around 577 AD.

There is a second school of thought, however, which subscribes to the theory that the tribe which first settled here, the *seo-mere-saetan* – the dwellers by the sea lakes – were responsible for naming the county.

Certainly, the Romans left their mark. The Fosse Way cuts right through the county from

*Left:* Excavating the Sweet Trackway.

Bath to Ilchester, an important town known by the Romans as *Lindinis* and the remains of several fine Roman villas have been found along its route.

Subsequently Somerset became a centre of Saxon culture and it was on an island amid the swamps at Athelney that King Alfred, whilst planning the defeat of the Danes, exhibited his complete lack of culinary skill and abused his landlady's hospitality by burning her cakes!

It was to Glastonbury, the ancient Isle of Avalon, and to a certain extent this is where legend takes over, that the first Christian missionaries came after the Crucifixion. Some sources even claim that the young Jesus Christ came regularly with his uncle, Joseph of Arimathea. Joseph is said to have returned after Christ's death, bearing the Holy Grail, the cup used at the 'Last Supper', which still reputedly lies hidden in the area. Joseph also brought with him two staffs, both of which he stuck in the ground and both turned into trees. One, the holy thorn, blossoms on old Christmas Day, 6 January, whilst the lesser

WEARY ALL HILL.

Weary All Hill, Glastonbury, with the tor in the background. The stone in the foreground is said to commemorate the date of Joseph of Arimathea's visit in AD 31. His companions were weary after their long journey from the Holy Land – hence the name.

known walnut flowers on St Barnabas Day, 11 June.

It is therefore not surprising that Glastonbury became the cradle of Christianity, with the Abbey growing in size over the centuries until, at 580 feet, it became the longest monastic church in the country. Its power and prosperity spread throughout the south of England and was only curbed at the dissolution of the monasteries in 1539. They could not do things by halves in those days; not only were the treasures stolen and the library vandalised, but the buildings became stone quarries, with local people using the stone to construct their own homes. Even today in their 'filleted' state, the ruins in which King Arthur and his Queen are said to have been buried, are magnificent.

I suppose the influence of the Abbey, coupled with the prosperous wool trade, explains why Somerset is richly endowed with so many fine buildings. The church

towers in particular, are splendid; built during the fifteenth century when wool made just about everyone rich.

They are Somerset's crowning glory covering the county from Dundry in the north to Huish Episcopi in the south; fingers of authority from a bygone age still soaring heavenwards to the glory of God.

Whole new towns developed as a result of this thriving wool trade, and on the Mendip hills at Mells is perhaps the finest. Today it is a large village, but its prosperous past is typified most of all by the glorious medieval church, built by those farmers and merchants, to show their appreciation to God for their fortune and prosperity.

Mells also has another claim to fame, for it was Little Jack Horner who sat in the corner of the office of Thomas Cromwell, when he was breaking up the monasteries for his master Henry VIII. A great supporter of Henry in all his policies, Horner put in 'his thumb and pulled out a plum', and that 'plum' was the Manor of Mells, valued at that time in 1548 at £1,831 19s 11¾d. So not only did Horner leave us with a nursery rhyme, but also the most beautiful small group of medieval buildings anywhere in the country.

The little street of medieval houses, leading directly to the churchyard entrance, is unique in itself, for they were the equivalent of a weekend cottage or commuters' house, as we know them today. They belonged to the merchants who, whilst they lived and worked mostly in London, Poole or Bristol, spent quite a fair portion of their time at Mells, when they organised the buying and selling of wool.

They quite sensibly built themselves dwellings in which to stay. If you think that a second house in the country is a modern innovation, then I am afraid you are wrong, because a second house was a custom of the rich fourteenth-century merchants.

The church entered the world of commerce in a big way, for the Abbots of Glastonbury were every bit as much businessmen as they were Christians, and when the two interests were combined glorious buildings like Wells Cathedral were erected. No words of mine are needed here to describe this wonderous place. Here it has stood for 700 years and here I feel sure it will stand for at least 700 more.

Tucked quietly away a stone's throw from the Cathedral, and linked to it by a bridge, is a fourteenth-century street, the

Church and manor house at Mells.

like of which you are unlikely to find anywhere. There are terraces of houses on left and right; all identically planned, they have now been subtly adapted by their owners, but in no way does this detract from its immense charm. Nearly 500 feet long, its width subtly decreases from south to north. Therefore you get an affect of forced perspective. It is a pity we cannot

Photograph of a splendid model of Glastonbury Abbey showing it in its heyday. Made by Nicholas Gaffney, it is on permanent display at the Abbey.

The Vicar's Close, Wells.

achieve such subtleties in some of today's stark architectural contributions.

They were built in 1348, and known as the Vicar's Close. The then Vicars of Wells were subordinate members of the Cathedral, and these were their quarters. Looking at them individually some are Georgian and some Victorian in character, and some have suffered from modernisation in the twentieth century, but in each case the general effect is good. I understand that the front gardens are comparatively modern, having been established in about 1420!

However, business transactions were not always conducted on church soil. Very often the monks erected special buildings for the storing and the bartering of wool. One such building is the George Inn at Norton St Philip: it was here the wool was stored and later auctioned. It was more of a dual purpose building, because apart from its connection with the wool trade, it was also a hostelry, run by the monks who could grant themselves licence to brew – and sell the results. Oh, what happy days! After all beer was a necessity to refresh the travellers and merchants who visited the monks to trade, for there were no proper public inns as we know them in those early days.

By the mid sixteenth century, when the profits from wool had multiplied, the Elizabethans built their now-famous manor houses and Montacute, on the outskirts of Yeovil, is probably one of, if not the, finest Elizabethan house in England.

The next milestone in Somerset's history came with the Georgians at Bath. There had been a settlement there since the Romans, but it was when Beau Nash popularised the city as a watering and gambling place, that the 'Jewel of the West' was born. Soon the finest architects of the time came to Bath to design, build and finally to live.

Perhaps the most famous group of buildings is the Royal Crescent, started in 1767 by John Wood, the younger, who was both architect and developer. It is a large half elipse, which at first sight appears to be perfect, similar to the effect created at the Vicar's Close in Wells, but if we look more closely, this is not the case.

Individual owners, during the succeeding years, have either changed the window shapes or window proportions, but nonetheless the overall effect remains. How monotonous it would have looked in a straight line. We should be eternally grateful

*Left:* Dundry Church tower.

*Right:* The George Inn, Norton St Philip.

*Above:* Roman Baths, at Bath.

*Below:* Royal Crescent at Bath.

Montacute House.

for the flash of brilliance which inspired John Wood, when he decided to bend it to the beautiful crescent shape.

We are told that Wood only designed the façade, and it was left to the individual purchaser to decide what happened behind. It is almost like walking round the back of a film set for a 'Western'. It is not exactly untidy, but the formality has disappeared and informality prevails; perhaps each owner at last had a chance to stamp his or her individuality on the original design.

There is every chance that Weston-super-Mare, together with the other resorts along the Somerset coastline, expanded from fishing villages to seaside towns, almost overnight as a direct consequence of the Napoleonic Wars. The great Continental resorts, having been closed to upper and middle-class holidaymakers, inspired them to seek solace along their own coastline. Certainly Weston, with its acres of muddy silt exposed by a sea which disappeared regularly with the turn of the tide, seems an unlikely candidate compared with, say, Brighton, but prosper it did. The arrival of the tide, complete with paddle steamers packed with day trippers from Wales and the railway in 1841, turned it into one of the most prosperous of our Westcountry resorts.

Inland towns prospered as well; by taking the 'waste' products of the sheep and cattle, thriving leather industries were set up in places like Street, Glastonbury and Yeovil. Gloves, shoes and sheepskin coats were, and are still being made, although in Yeovil the town's prosperity revolves around the helicopter, rather than the glove.

The county has had its share of bloodshed over the centuries; varying from a slight skirmish during the Civil War at Babylon Hill, between Yeovil Roundheads and Sherborne Cavaliers, to hosting on Sedgemoor the last battle to be fought by Englishmen on English soil. There in 1685 the Monmouth Rebellion was put down and many sons of Somerset brutally put to the sword. From that moment it seems that the county turned away from involvement in national affairs, concentrating all of its energy on the things that really matter – the making of cream, butter, cheese and, of course, cider!

The muster of Roundheads in St John's Churchyard, Yeovil, prior to the Battle of Babylon Hill, questionably the slightest of skirmishes to take place during the whole of the Civil War. This is the only known copy of a painting by Dorset artist, Francis Newbery, as the original was destroyed in the Town Hall fire of 1935.

North Street, Taunton, at or about the end of Edward VII's reign.

Taunton, the county town, is thought to date from about the year 700 when it was founded by King Ina. He built a fine castle here to defend his kingdom from the Welsh. This made him the first Saxon king with any power; power which he used in an attempt to unify this part of England for the first time since the Romans left.

Pre 1905 view of double deck tramcar at Burmah Cross
in Taunton.

Trams failed to survive long in Taunton. In 1901 a one-and-a-half-mile route in the town centre was opened using double-deck vehicles (*left*). The system closed in 1905 when the foundations of the track collapsed. After rebuilding, the system re-opened using single deck cars (*below*). Following a dispute with the corporation, who supplied the electric power, the plug was pulled out in 1921 and the Taunton Electric Traction Co. Ltd, who had refused to pay the higher charges, became the second tramway in the county to close.

The fine half-timbered house in the centre of this view of
Taunton stands in the middle of a group of sixteenth-century
town houses. Seen to advantage today because of our modern
wide streets, such houses originally overhung the streets
below so much that people could often shake hands with their
neighbours opposite from the top storey.

The Castle Hotel, formerly Clarke's Hotel, looking much older
than it really is, provides a grand architectural complement to
the adjoining castle, which now houses the fine county
museum.

Bridgwater, one of Somerset's more industrialised towns, stands on the River Parrett. It is notable for its bore, a tidal wave which comes up twice a day with the tidal waters, the effect of which can be felt practically as far inland as Langport.

*The Bridge from Salmon Parade, Bridgwater, Somerset.*

*Right:* Bridgwater in the late 1860s. The small paddle tug on the left is the *Petrel*, owned by G.B. Sully of Bridgwater. Built in 1863 this little wooden vessel was 81 feet long and 71 gross tons. In 1866 she ran excursions from Watchet to Bristol and Avonmouth. The silting up of the river can clearly be seen.

Fire appliances of the day parading through Bridgwater on the
occasion of the launching of the lifeboat.

LIFEBOAT DAY 1908

*Left:* Cornhill, Bridgwater, showing open-top bus.

Barquentine berthed at the docks at Bridgwater in 1895, an
area now being developed as a marina.

Bridgwater cattle market at Penel Orlieu. It moved to Bath
Road in 1935.

I do not suppose you can have been born and then lived in a county without finding traces of relatives somewhere along the line. This picture of the vicar and choir of St Mary's Parish Church, Bridgwater (*left*), was taken in 1908 and the chorister on the extreme left of the front row is my late father-in-law, Leonard Hole, a former mayor of Yeovil.

The discovery of this picture prompted me to search for traces of other relatives among photographs available within the county. The one *below* shows my great grandfather, Fred Young, lending his support to Lizzie Little, winner of a donkey race during Queen Victoria's Jubilee celebrations in Yeovil. He is third from the right in the rakish bowler.

Carnivals have always been popular in the county, particularly at Bridgwater, so I was not really surprised to find my father-in-law popping up again as a contestant in the 'Dunball Treacle Mines Championship'. They only took third prize and that's him hiding his disappointment in the back row behind the tiny umbrella.

I fancy Miss 'Made in England' (*left*), who wasn't among the prize winners, is about to show her disappointment with a tear or two – the corners of her mouth are definitely drooping!

Among a collection of photographs taken of various floats in the Yeovil carnival of 1922 I found another Fred Young (*left*), this one my father, dressed as Bill Sykes on the Three Choughs' Hotel's 'Tribute to Dickens' float. I reckon, by the look of him in the photograph taken after the event (*below left*) that he'd had a good day!

*Below:* My father-in-law makes one final unscheduled appearance in this unique photograph of a complete farm removal by special train from Lodge Station, Glastonbury. He was apparently station master there. That's him on the right of the trio. The move took place in 1937.

Interior view of Buncombe's works, Highbridge. This company hired out steam rollers in the Somerset area. A collection like this is unlikely to be ever seen again.

Although for centuries drains were dug and sea walls built on the Somerset levels, many under the patronage of the monks at Glastonbury, it wasn't until recent times, under the auspices of the former Somerset River Authority, that serious attempts were made to drain the Levels.

This photograph, taken in the early 1920s, shows how serious flooding was in the Glastonbury area, with the train as well as Glastonbury Tor virtually in splendid isolation.

*Left:* Aveling and Porter 8 ton roller built in 1930 working in Bridgwater Docks. By the late 1950s the steam roller was a dying breed but this lucky chap has been preserved.

Reconstructed view of Glastonbury Lake village.

*Below:* This picture of the main Abbey Church at Glastonbury was taken from the position of the high altar back in 1904. Fortunately the picturesque but damaging trees and ivy covering the walls has long since gone.

*Left:* Life must have been difficult in the Iron Age lake villages on the Somerset Levels. This reconstructed view of life as it was in the Glastonbury village (*left*) shows how most communication was by water.

*Right:* Old Wells Road, Glastonbury, taken at the turn of the century. There is a theory that not all of the stone from the Abbey was taken by locals to build their own houses at the Dissolution of the Monasteries; much of it, it is claimed, was used to construct the road over the Levels between Glastonbury and Wells.

*Left:* A closer view of Glastonbury Tor taken from lower down Weary All Hill.

Glastonbury, Wells Old Road.

*Right:* One of the most popular day trips in the early 1920s was
to the Cheddar Caves when everyone sat five abreast with a
separate door at the end of each row of seats. Note the great
'pram' hood stacked at the back, ready to be passed hand-
over-hand to the front at the slightest hint of rain.

*Left:* King John's Shooting Box, or Hunting Lodge, as it is known today, has no connection with King John, despite the fact that he was responsible for granting Axbridge a certain degree of independence during his reign. Today this fine half-timbered merchant's house, for that is what it was, contains a museum and is run by The National Trust.

Illumination by electricity miraculously transformed Gough's Caves at Cheddar. What a pity they had to spoil the illusion with so many trailing cables.

The appropriately named Lion Rock looming over the Rose
Cottage Tea Rooms at Cheddar Gorge in the 1920s.

It is generally considered that the natural spring water in the pool at the Bishop's Palace, pictured (*right*) in 1897, gave Wells its name – the minster by the spring.

*Below:* A rare early aerial photograph of Wells and the Cathedral taken in 1925.

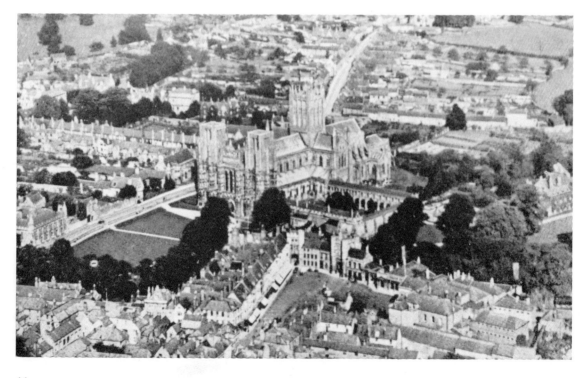

Wells marketplace is a hand down through the ages of an almost perfect Medieval square. This picture taken at the turn of the century shows it in all its glory mercifully free of the motorcar which, by virtue of its presence in ever increasing numbers, detracts from its beauty today. Notwithstanding that, it is for me, the finest square in Europe, with the Piazza San Marco, Venice, coming a close second.

*Left:* The famous bell-ringing swans on the moat which surrounds the Bishop's Palace at Wells. The caption on the postcard tells us that Miss Eden, daughter of Lord Auckland, Bishop of Bath and Wells from 1854-69, first taught the swans to ring a bell placed beneath the window from which she threw food to them.

Downside Abbey with its public school stands beside the Fosseway at Stratton-on-the-Fosse. It was founded in 1607, although many of the buildings are of more recent date. This bird's eye view is from an architectural perspective. The abbey nave has the distinction of being designed by architect Sir Giles Gilbert Scott in 1923.

This view of Stoneaston is taken from a postcard dated 1926.
The message written to a friend in Bath is interesting for it
draws attention to the fact that the writer is featured in the
picture. She's the one in the hat behind the wall on the left.

*Right:* Famous for its stone circles, Stanton Drew can also boast
this fine octagonal toll house with its thatched roof – octagonal
because such a shape, whilst difficult to live in, did provide
all-round visibility to spot approaching coaches, many of
which tried to 'gate crash', thus avoiding paying a toll. To stop
this happening a row of pikes were often fixed to the gate in an
upright position. They were turned horizontally at the
approach of a vehicle – hence the term 'turn pike' – which soon
stopped them in their tracks.

For once it's not oil slicks on the road here at Chilcompton, but the waste products of real horse power! Waste products which were far from wasted, for many a stick of rhubarb benefited.

The Circus, Bath.

The Circus at Bath, or the King's Circus as it was originally
known, dates from 1754 when the work was first started. The
design is fascinating for the coupled columns on the fronts are
in three different Roman orders of architecture: Tuscan, Ionic
and Corinthian.

*Right:* 'Taking the waters at Bath' – literally.

The King's Bath in the Roman Baths at Bath.

*Right:* 'Guinea Pig Jack', a well-known Bath character, who made his living selling guinea pigs in the streets at Bath. By the shape of his trousers I should think he kept a few spares in them as well as in his basket.

Milsom Street, Bath, seen here just prior to the First World War, was begun in 1762 and designed by John Wood, the elder.

Two contrasting forms of Bath transport, the mail coach and
the tram. Electric trams had replaced horse trams at Bath by
1904; the forty trams in the fleet were painted pale blue and
cream. In 1936 the system was acquired by Bristol Tramways
and a complete change to motor buses made by 6 May 1939, the
day that the last tram ran.

The London, Bath, and Bristol Night Coach (1838), taking up Roadside Mails
without halting.

*Left:* High Street, Bath, in 1899, complete with trams.

A variety of transport in Somerset. *Right:* The National bus service between Crewkerne and Yeovil taken in 1921. I wonder why the driver needed the support of two 'clippies' – after all it was only a single decker?

Surely the most unusual bicycle 'made for two' ever conceived. Supplied by Hyde & Wakely of Yeovil, it is really a form of motorcycle, known as a tricar, which explains the registration 'Y 242' on the side of the passenger seat. The cycles in the window are priced from £10.10.0.

Sully's Bus Company of Chard – part of a line-up of vehicles
mainly of Dennis and Leyland manufacture. This local
company was acquired by Southern National in 1936.

Another form of passenger transport. The upper photograph
is of the *Glen Avon*, a Campbell's paddle steamer, off Weston-
super-Mare on 15 August 1937. Built in 1912 she served in two
world wars, but in September 1944 she was lost off the French
coast. In the background *Cambria*, built in 1895, also served in
both wars and was broken up in 1946 being beyond repair. In
the lower picture Campbell's steamer *Albion* is ashore on
Blacknose Rock, Portishead, on April fool's day 1907. Built in
1893 she was successfully refloated and eventually sold
in 1921.

The railway made its impression on the landscape in more
ways than one. This viaduct at Pensford, with its sixteen
arches built of stone and brick in 1873, dominates the village
which was the focal point for three small coal mines. Pensford
Colliery closed in 1958.

The Viaduct, Pensford.

High Street                    Shepton Mallett

The market cross dating from 1500 fills the centre of Shepton
Mallet's marketplace. The town is yet another example of a
place which prospered through the wool trade. No doubt its
position as a communications centre added to that early
prosperity, making it, for a while, the focus of the cloth trade
in this part of Somerset.

Market Place, Shepton Mallett.

*Left:* At the time this photograph of Shepton Mallet High Street was taken the town was considered to be the centre of the Cheddar cheese industry. Shepton is thought to be short for Sheep Town whilst Mallett most certainly comes from the Malet family, Lords of the Manor in Norman times.

The pond at Castle Cary, now graced by the war memorial, was here before the manor house which stood next to it; like the castle it too has disappeared. Parson Woodforde, the diaryist, was Rector of Ansford and Vicar of Castle Cary. It is his record of life in those simple days, and that of his son James, which still continues to fascinate many of us today.

This horse was stolen at Wincanton and the man responsible was the last one in Britain to be hanged for horse stealing. Unfortunately details of the offence and the name of the offender are unknown.

*Right:* The lifeblood of every village was the village pump. This photograph of Templecombe village pump was taken at the turn of the century.

Templecombe was once owned and occupied by the Knights
Templar. Some of the barns, including one in which they ate,
are still standing. The great treasure is in the church; it is a
wooden panel with the painted face of Christ, displayed in
such a way that many experts have remarked on its similarity
to the face on the Turin shroud.

# FRED COOPER,

## TAILOR AND HABIT MAKER,

### Clothier, Hatter & Juvenile Outfitter.

SEPARATE ROOM

APPROPRIATED TO THE

## Juvenile Department.

### BOYS' SUITS

IN ALL THE

### NEWEST & LEADING STYLES.

The Ready-made Department

IS REPLETE WITH AN EXTENSIVE
ASSORTMENT OF

## GENTLEMEN'S SUITS,
### OVERCOATS, &c.

☞ GRATIS—With all Purchases of Shirting Flannel, we give a well-tested Paper Shirt Pattern, cut upon the latest principles.

In consequence of the large increase in his Bespoke Trade, F. C. respectfully announces his having devoted a SPECIAL ROOM to his TAILORING DEPARTMENT.

A CHOICE SELECTION OF WOOLLENS.

## LADIES' JACKETS MADE TO ORDER.

Patterns and Rules for Self-Measurement Post Free.

## The West of England Outfitting Establishment,
# 16, HIGH STREET, YEOVIL.
## ALSO AT WINCHESTER AND BASINGSTOKE.

Taken in 1878 this photograph of Yeovil shows us how everyone stopped for the photographer in those early days. Close examination of the picture shows us that the lad looking round in the road is wearing a black mourning band. The lad just opposite him on the pavement to the left of the picture has toothache, for his jowl is bandaged up, with the bandage obviously tied on top of his head and tucked under his cap.

*Left:* Who says that advertisements in years gone by weren't adequate? This one, taken from Whitby & Son's *Yeovil Almanack Advertiser* of 1885, not only tells the story but tells it in seventeen different sets of type!

*Left:* 'Kitchener's Army' parading through the centre of Yeovil on their way to the western front.

The Prince of Wales, later Edward VIII, riding on Yeovil's first motor fire engine on a visit to the town in 1923.

*Right:* Rare photograph of political rally taken at the Triangle, Yeovil, in 1911, with the parliamentary candidate, Aubrey Herbert, addressing a crowd of supporters. The lads on the fringe of the crowd are more interested in the photographer and possible press coverage than the speaker – times don't change do they? Incidentally, isn't it interesting that everyone wore a hat in those days – perhaps we do change with the times after all?

Middle Street, Yeovil, showing the Castle Hotel, a former chantry, now demolished. The photograph taken in 1905 shows the horse-drawn omnibus on its way from the railway station to the major hotels in the town.

Aubrey Herbert won the Yeovil seat in the 1911 election, going forward to contest the seat again after the First World War.

Polling Day, December 14th.

*The favour of your Vote
is solicited for*

**Lt.-Col. Hon. Aubrey Herbert**
(Irish Guards).

*He has been your Member
since 1911,
and has done his best to serve you
both in
Peace and WAR.*

Printed and Published by E. Whitby & Son,
Albion Printing Works, Yeovil.

*Right:* Those were the 'Sunday School' days. It was not just the trade unions which sported their 'colours' at the turn of the century, but everybody else, Sunday Schools included.

*Left:* Matron and staff plus the odd patient or two at Yeovil's
first hospital at Fiveways taken in 1909.

*Right:* An early picture taken about 1922 of Yeovil and Petter's United, vanguard of Yeovil's giant-killing football teams of later years.

*Left:* The Yeovil Constabulary taken about seventy years ago –
up to full strength, all 23 of them, plus the mascot in the centre
of the picture between the Police Chief's feet!

It seems only right that the Westland Aircraft Company should have developed in Somerset at Yeovil, for it was at nearby Chard in 1847 that John Stringfellow made the first flight in an aeroplane that he had built. Sadly, he received little glory for his efforts, despite the fact that his plane flew the length of Crystal Palace in 1868, lifting several feet into the air the wire to which it was tethered. Unfortunately for him it was only possible to heat the engine by methylated spirit – and the flame kept blowing out. Thus by such small margins do men miss out on greatness – he ended his days almost penniless making bobbins for Chard's net industry. Today he is probably the most revered of all the pioneers of flight.

*Right:* Accidents happen even in the best regulated circles as this picture shows. This aircraft made a premature landing in the allotments on the perimeter of Westlands Airfield.

The story of the Westland Aircraft Company, really the story of aviation in this country, is well told elsewhere; suffice it for me to say that since the early 1920s, when it was just a small extension to Petters world-renowned oil engines, with 50 employees, it has become one of the world's largest helicopter manufacturers.

*Left:* This was the total staff employed by the Woodmill Department at Westland Aircraft at the end of the First World War in 1918; a complete contrast to the many thousands employed there today. The aircraft behind them is a de Havilland 9A.

*Below:* One of Westland Helicopters Ltd early helicopters, the Westland Dragonfly.

*Right:* Between the first and second World Wars, the Westland Aircraft Company were constantly experimenting with new aircraft. The Pterodactyl was a much discussed experimental aircraft which flew but was never mass-produced.

The Westland Lysander was probably the finest aircraft to emerge from the Westland Aircraft Company during the Second World War and one which played an important part in that conflict.

The three-engined, six-seater Westland Wessex plane was used as the first passenger service aircraft in the Westcountry. That first flight took place between Plymouth and Cardiff on 12 April 1933 and was operated by the Great Western Railway.

The Roman villa at Lufton discovered in 1945. This is a
reconstruction drawn by L.E.J. Brooke from a model by
D. Kettlety in Yeovil Museum. Lufton is between Yeovil
and Ilchester.

*Right:* A fish mozaic in an octagonal bath at Lufton Villa. Note
the fish blowing bubbles.

Mosaic medallion forming part of a tessellated pavement found at Lufton Villa.

*Left:* High Ham windmill, built in 1822, has now been restored to its former glory by The National Trust. This photograph, taken in 1910, shows it in its heyday complete with thatched roof. This gentle giant from the past is one of the most functional buildings ever to have been designed and a masterpiece of technology in its own time.

This particular picture is one of a series of postcards issued by St Ivel, makers of 'St Ivel cheese, butter, cream, jellies, potted meats and the exotic calves' tongues in glass' to quote their publicity on the back of the card. This particular view, packed with dairy produce providers, shows the garden front of Brympton d'Evercy. Brympton with its house, church and gardens is one of the finest architectural groups to be found in the Westcountry.

The building of Montacute House was started about 1590 by
Thomas Phelips and completed by his son, Sir Edward, the
Speaker of the House of Commons at the time when Guy
Fawkes was making his attempt to put the world, as well as
Parliament, to rights.

The Phelips lived here for 300 years; it was subsequently
leased to Lord Curzon and finally given to the nation,
becoming one of the finest jewels in the crown of The
National Trust.

*Right:* The Square, or Borough as it is known in Montacute,
really is a square, loomed over by St Michael's Hill, site of a
former Norman castle. The steep hill (or mons acutus) is
thought to be the derivation for the name Montacute.

Montacute Castle was built by the Count of Mortain, half-brother of William the Conquerer. By building it on St Michael's Hill, he was desecrating holy ground, for fragments of the Holy Cross had reputedly been found there, thus in its way strengthening the Glastonbury claim of Joseph of Arimathea's presence in Somerset.

To atone for his desecration, he founded a priory below the hill. Little now remains of the buildings except the fine gatehouse, now Abbey Farm farmhouse.

*Right:* Rare early air photograph of South Petherton, showing
the Parish Church of SS Peter and Paul, much of which dates
from the thirteenth century and earlier.

*Left:* This is the full complement of staff at Stoke-under-Ham (or Stoke-sub-Hamdon as it is known today) taken some time during the reign of King Edward VII. The clue is the recruiting poster and the E.R. postbox.

I love the hats, particularly as worn by the bearded postman in the centre of the picture; he looks more like an infantryman from the American Civil War. Note the early Somerset registration Y.367 on the post office van.

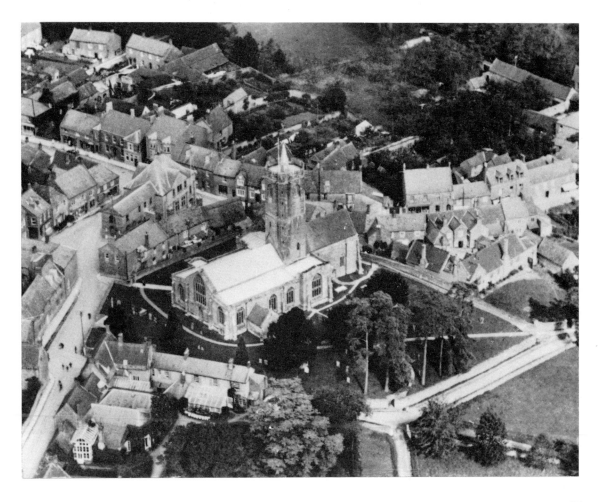

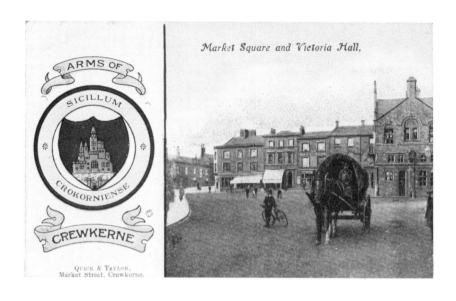

North Perrott, taken in April 1905. Note the horse trough side-
by-side with the village pump.

*Left:* This was a trade card issued by a local trader, probably by the firm whose cart is featured in the picture. Crewkerne, famous for its St Bartholomew's Fair, dating from about 1270, which still regularly spills into the streets during the month of June, can trace its origins back to Saxon times when the town boasted a mint and market.

Family group taken outside the village store and post office at West Chinnock, near Crewkerne in 1906. Note the village pump, complete with bucket, the only water supply at that time.

Rare picture of Chard Central station formerly known as
'Chard Joint' opened with a branch from Taunton on
11 September 1866 – a typical Bristol & Exeter Railway design
of the period. Later this company was acquired by the GWR
and the branch remained broad gauge until 1891, a year before
its final withdrawal to stop the LSWR pressing for running
powers between Chard Town LSWR station and Taunton.

*Right:* Langport East – opened on 2 July 1906. With the
completion of the Castle Cary to Taunton cut-off line, this, the
last new main line in the Westcountry, cut over 20 miles off the
route to the west. Prior to this all Great Western trains travelled
via Bristol.

The Great Western Railway were pioneers in the use of diesel railcars for branch lines (above at Cheddar Station) long before the development of the diesel train by British Railways.

Somerset's own railway was the Somerset & Dorset, a line of outstanding interest and many books have appeared covering the history of the line. Here goods locomotive no. 53807, one of a class of eleven heavy freight engines built to handle the coal traffic, enters Radstock. In the background is a spoil tip and to the right of the signal box the tunnel of the old Somerset coal canal tramway.

*Right:* Before the closure of the Somerset coalfield, many small mines existed and were served by railways to transport the coal. Seen here at Kilmersdon Colliery is a Somerset engine built in 1929 by Peckett of Bristol. She spent her life at Norton Hill and later at Kilmersdon pits shunting wagons. She is now preserved by the Somerset & Dorset Railway Trust at Washford Station.

S. & D. (Slow & Doubtful) Railway
Wincanton to Bath

The Somerset & Dorset Railway had to put up with a degree of
cynicism in its day, summed up by this rather 'unkind'
postcard. In some circles the 'Doubtful' in 'Slow & Doubtful'
was substituted for 'Dirty'. Very unkind when you consider
they had more steep inclines than just about any other
operating railway.

*Right:* The county has had its share of railway accidents, particularly in the south of the county. On 3 July 1914 Yeovil Junction's west signal box took a serious tumble.

Situated on high ground above Radstock, a cable-worked incline was used to transport wagons to and from the GWR Frome-Radstock branch. Full wagons going down on the left hauled up empty wagons on the right by means of the cables seen in the foreground and controlled by a brake drum at the top of the incline. This is the last of its type to be used in the country.

On 8 August 1913 the Weymouth Express crashed into the rear of a passenger train at Pen Mill Station and three people were killed. A little memorium card was produced (*right*) containing a poem specially written to commemorate the sad event with the proceeds going to the local hospital. What a gentler age it must have been when tragedies like this were glorified by such tributes. Today we have no time for such eloquence, merely a front page display of the most dramatic picture obtainable.

*Right:* Aqueduct at Creech St Michael which carried the Taunton to Chard canal, opened in 1842. Later it was closed and allowed to become derelict by the Bristol & Exeter Railway Company.

THE time of the year had arrived,
  When those who from toil could be freed,
    To visit their friends, and some pleasure
      derive,
  And a rest, such as all of us need.

The journey begins, and their friends
  Who are waiting to welcome their kin,
Know the time of their journey by rail soon
  ends,
    And the train, with their loved ones,
      steams in.

But oh! how uncertain is life!
  Long or short, with its dangers so near,
For we "know not the hour" when accidents
  rife
    Shall befall us, and end our career.

The ill-fated train was at rest
  At the platform discharging her freight,
When in serpent-like form came the heavy
  express
    Round the curve, like a thief in the night.

Then the crash! then the piteous cries
  Of the wounded, the crushed and the
    maimed.
Then a piercing "God help me" ascends to
  the skies,
    And willing hands succour the lamed.

The skilled in "first aid" soon began
  To help till the doctors arrived,
But alas! some had ended this mortal life's
  span,
    And some were but barely alive.

But nobly did doctors work on,
  With matron and nurses as well,
Yea, all who had helped till the work had
  been done,
    Deserve all the praise we can tell.

May such scenes ever prompt us to cry:
  "Lord, teach us to number our days";
That we "unto wisdom our hearts may apply,"
  And for *our* preservation give praise.

Yeovil.                                    J. Tupman.

---

*Proceeds of this to be given to the Yeovil Hospital*

Published by L. J. Fox, Stationer, Yeovil.

Some sons of Somerset. Somerset has produced its fair share of
famous sons from St Dunstan of Glastonbury to Yeovilian Ian
Botham.

St Dunstan, like so many great men, was multi-talented;
musician, sculptor, metalworker, illustrator of manuscripts
and folksong writer. He was made Abbot of Glastonbury in
943 and eventually Archbishop of Canterbury in 959.

Somerset's most amazing son must surely be Friar Roger
Bacon, philosopher and scientist, who was born in the
Ilchester area on or about the year 1220. He discovered the use
of lenses and could therefore possibly be described as the
inventor of spectacles. He travelled much of the then known
world accurately prophesying the invention of ocean
steamers, railways, motorcars, flying machines, cranes, even
suspension bridges. All these centuries before the reputedly
greatest inventor of all time – Leonardo da Vinci. I wonder
whether he picked up his ideas from this renowned
Somerset monk?

Over the years men of Somerset have explored the world: Tom Coryate, was known as the 'Odcombe legstretcher'. Son of the vicar, he walked almost everywhere, throughout Europe and Asia Minor, hence his nickname. Most of his journeys were made during the first decade of the seventeenth century and he is credited with re-introducing the use of the fork at the meal table. A pair of his shoes hung for many years in the church until one was stolen; the remaining shoe is today in the vicar's safekeeping.

William Dampier of East Coker, navigator and buccaneer, was sent by the Admiralty on a voyage of discovery around the coast of Australia way back in 1699. It was he who punished one of his junior officers, Alexander Selkirk, by putting him ashore on a lonely Pacific island. He was much surprised to find him still alive years later, so he brought him home where he was immortalised by Daniel Defoe in his famous story *Robinson Crusoe*.

Langport's greatest son was Walter Bagehot, the nineteenth century economist. An authority on finance and the English constitution, his scholarship was such that he was forever being consulted by the government of the day, whatever the party.

MR HENRY IRVING

PIGGOTT.

Nor was Somerset backward in producing exponents of the performing arts; Sir Henry Irving questionably England's finest actor, was born at Keinton Mandeville in 1838. My picture of him sporting a boater with 'Piggott', is a tintype; a seaside photograph rather like our polaroid pictures today. After it was taken, it was then mounted, albeit roughly.

Irving must have been about fourteen when this unique photograph was taken, dating it at about 1852. Obviously the young Henry was very much the gentleman with his fob and watch chain, whilst his unknown companion 'Piggott' was quite possibly his tutor.

Milverton's great son was probably the most precocious genius to have ever lived for, by the age of fourteen, this talented lad had written his autobiography – in Latin!

Thomas Young developed into one of the most profound minds that the world has ever seen: for his thinking in mathematical physics determined the course of scientific thought throughout the nineteenth century. Apart from his brilliant skills as a doctor and anatomist, it is as an Egyptologist that he is best known. He was responsible for decoding the mysteries of Egyptian hieroglyphs and by so doing opened up for us all the fascinating panorama of Egyptian history.

It seems logical for Dulverton, lying as it does south of Exmoor, to have prospered from the wool trade. Streams running off the moor powered mills which treated woollen cloth produced from the moorland sheep. Dulverton's most famous son, Sir George Williams was born on the outskirts of the town. He founded the YMCA in 1844.

*Right:* There's no doubt about it, they really could strike a bargain in the old days; apparently in 1442 the people of Dunster contracted with builder John Marys to construct the 100 foot tower at the rate of 13s 4d per foot, with an additional £1 being paid for the four pinnacles at the top. By my reckoning the tower cost them £67 13s 4d – a bargain by anyone's standards.

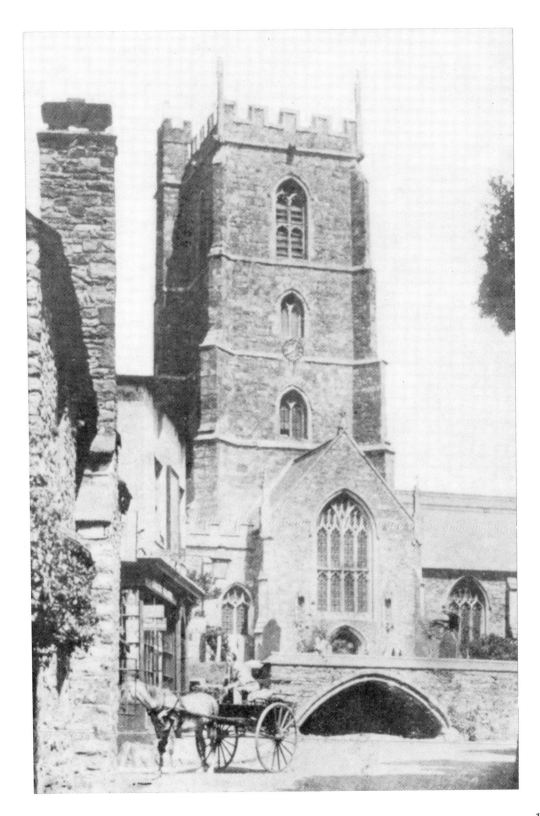

Wootton Courtnay lies under Exmoor with its saddleback
tower an unusual feature in a Somerset church.

Wotton Courtnay Church,

*Left:* Dunster's wide main street is dominated by the Yarn Market and has been ever since it was completed in 1589, although substantial repairs were made to this market cross, with its strange roof shape, in 1647. The circular tower on Conygar Hill is often mistaken as the castle.

*Above:* The old Nunnery in Church Street Dunster, was no such thing. Far from it, for it was owned by the Abbots of Cleeve. This delightful building, much of it dating from the fourteenth century, is hung with shiny slates which glitter like fish scales on a sunny day.

Oare Church was made famous by R.D. Blackmore in his novel
*Lorna Doone*. Such is the power of the book that many people
think that the events really took place – an illusion supported
by the graves of several Ridds in the churchyard.

Porlock Weir.

It was in the Ship Inn at Porlock that poet, Robert Southey, wrote his immortal lines, two of which sum up for me the whole concept of the English seaside holiday.

'Porlock! I shall not forget thee,
Here by the unwelcome summer rain confined.'

*Above:* This delightful picture postcard showing Porlock's truncated church spire, which lost its head in a thunder storm, has a message written on the back which shows implicit faith in the efficiency of the post office in 1904, for it reads as follows: 'Dear Dorothy, I am sorry I shall not be able to be with you today but mother is ill, Love Eileen.' Apparently same day post, even of a postcard with a halfpenny stamp on it was not unusual, even, as in this case, between Porlock and Bristol!

North Hill & Promenade Minehead

*Right:* Watchet, renowned as the home of paper manufacturers since the 1600s, can claim greater fame as the port from which Coleridge's *Ancient Mariner* set sail. 'Here is where he shall set out on his fateful voyage' are his reputed words to Wordsworth as he saw Watchet – looking very much as it does in this picture – when he saw it for the first time on a walk from Nether Stowey to Lynton.

*Left:* Minehead started life as a Bristol Channel port and like its sister ports along the Somerset coastline modestly took in lodgers in the shape of summer visitors seeking seaside seclusion away from the hordes who flocked to the south coast at the turn of the century.

Combwich was the outport of Bridgwater during the Middle Ages. This photograph taken in 1910 illustrates the variety of topography to be found in Somerset for this could easily be East Anglia or even Holland.

Why is it you never seem to come across people featured in postcards? Certainly the sender of this card seemed to recognise someone on this seat on Burnham Esplanade, as the pencilled message on the front of the card implies. Or was it just a keen sense of humour?

A first dip at Weston-super-Mare during the summer of 1912 and it looks as if the budding naturist is really enjoying herself!

This delightful postcard showing Weston's famous donkeys
has a rather cryptic message on the back which asks for a reply
by return of post 'as to whether the white washing is done'.
Some people can't relax even when they are on holiday!

*Left:* The pier pavilion, Weston-super-Mare.

Who says that beaches weren't crowded in the 'good' old days? I wonder if the lady gesticulating in the foreground of the postcard was telling off the lad centre right for picking his nose? If he was, you can't blame him for there doesn't appear to be much room to do anything else on the beach!

The entrance to Portishead pier with one of the 'White Funnel' fleet making its approach to disembark her complement of day trippers from Wales.

*Left:* It wasn't all sunshine at Weston-super-Mare. This fine photograph, taken at the turn of the century, was made into an attractive Christmas card.

It was not all sunshine and sand at the seaside as this winter
picture taken in 1908 at Clevedon shows.

*Left:* Clevedon Pier, probably the most elegant pier ever
designed, suffered storm damage but is now being restored to
its former glory.

# Also Available

**AROUND GLORIOUS DEVON**
by David Young

**EXMOOR IN THE OLD DAYS**
by Rosemary Anne Lauder

**LEGENDS OF SOMERSET**
by Sally Jones

**STRANGE SOMERSET STORIES**
Introduced by David Foot

**VIEWS OF OLD DEVON**
by Rosemary Anne Lauder

**VIEWS OF OLD PLYMOUTH**
by Sarah Foot

**THE CORNISH COUNTRYSIDE**
by Sarah Foot

**SEA STORIES OF DEVON**
Introduced by E.V. Thompson

**SEA STORIES OF CORNWALL**
by Ken Duxbury

**MOUNT'S BAY**
by Douglas Williams

**DARTMOOR IN THE OLD DAYS**
by James Mildren

**100 YEARS ON BODMIN MOOR**
by E.V. Thompson

**LEGENDS OF DEVON**
by Sally Jones

**GHOSTS OF DEVON**
by Peter Underwood

**UNKNOWN DEVON**
Rosemary Anne Lauder, Michael Williams &
Monica Wyatt

**UNKNOWN CORNWALL**
by Michael Williams

**NORTH CORNWALL IN THE OLD DAYS**
by Joan Rendell

**CURIOSITIES OF DEVON**
by Michael Williams

**ALONG THE DART**
by Judy Chard

**ALONG THE TEIGN**
by Judy Chard

**GHOSTS OF CORNWALL**
by Peter Underwood

**LEGENDS OF CORNWALL**
by Sally Jones

We shall be pleased to send you our catalogue giving
full details of our growing list of titles for Devon,
Cornwall and Somerset and forthcoming publications.

If you have difficulty in obtaining our titles, write
direct to Bossiney Books, Land's End, St Teath,
Bodmin, Cornwall.